THEY WRITE THEIR OWN SENTENCES

NORTH CAROLINA
STATE BOARD OF COMMUNITY COLLEGES
LIBRARIES
SAMPSON COMMUNITY COLLEGE

THEY WRITE THEIR OWN SENTENCES

The FBI Handwriting Analysis Manual

PALADIN PRESS
BOULDER, COLORADO

They Write Their Own Sentences:
The FBI Handwriting Analysis Manual

Copyright © 1987 by Paladin Press

ISBN 0-87364-446-8
Printed in the United States of America

Published by Paladin Press, a division of
Paladin Enterprises, Inc., P.O. Box 1307,
Boulder, Colorado 80306, USA.
(303)443-7250

Direct inquiries and/or orders to the above address.

All rights reserved. Except for use in a review, no
portion of this book may be reproduced in any form
without the express written permission of the publisher.

Neither the author nor the publisher assumes
any responsibility for the use or misuse of
information contained in this book.

Reprinted from the FBI Law Enforcement Bulletin

THEY WRITE THEIR OWN SENTENCES

Table of Contents

The FBI Laboratory	1
The Document Section	1
National Fraudulent Check File	4
Checkwriter Standards File	4
Safety Paper Standards File	4
Rubber Stamps and Printing Standards File	4
Typewriter Standards File	4
Anonymous Letter File	5
Watermark File	5
Submission of Evidence	6
The Check Passer	9
The National Fraudulent Check File	10
Examination of Checks	11
Other Specimens	13
Forgery of Genuine Signature	15
Mechanically Made Checks	17
Obtaining Known Specimens	19
Rubber Stamps	20
Documentary Evidence	25
Submission of Evidence	26
Types of Examinations	27
Physical Characteristics	28
Concealed Clues	32
Indented Writing	33
Transferred Writing	35
Alterations and Obliterations	37
Handwriting Examination	40
Anonymous Letters	42
Disguised Writing	42
Handwriting Comparisons	43

SCIENTIFIC AIDS

They Write Their Own Sentences

FBI LABORATORY'S DOCUMENT SECTION

The FBI Laboratory

The FBI Laboratory, an organization which now has almost unlimited scientific resources for criminal investigation at its disposal, started in 1932 with one microscope and one examiner. However, the main purpose of the Laboratory--to be of service not only to our own Special Agents in their investigations, but also to city, county, State and Federal law enforcement agencies all over the United States-- has remained unchanged. Thanks to the cooperation given the FBI by these law enforcement agencies, this purpose has to a great extent been achieved.

The Document Section

The Document Section of the FBI Laboratory is often regarded as primarily concerned with handwriting examinations, but the field of document work is considerably more extensive. The examinations of documents involve not only handwriting and handprinting, but typewriting, checkwriter impressions, rubber-stamp impressions, watermarks, printing methods, obliterations, alterations, paper and ink examinations, special photographic processes, charred paper--in fact, almost any type of examination that can be made of a piece of paper. The work of the Document Section is not limited to paper evidence, however, as this section also examines many types of evidence used in the preparation of documents, as well as various articles which bear handwriting or other forms of lettering or printing. Thus, it is not unusual for a document examiner to handle such things as used typewriter ribbons, lead printing dies, stolen suitcases from which identifying initials have been removed, wooden crates bearing obliterated addresses, etc.

Sometimes documentary evidence submitted to the Laboratory presents its own peculiar problem which can be solved only by the application of new techniques, and research on such problems is conducted by the Document Section in addition to its regular examinations. For example, considerable work has been done during the past few years in the field of

Figure 1

invisible radiations as applied to the problem of bringing up obliterated and altered writings, or writings which are indistinct because of age, charring, or other reasons. Through experiments with infrared, ultraviolet, and X-ray photography, good results have been obtained in many such cases. As an illustration, infrared photography was primarily responsible for the conviction of four Maryland "bookies" who tried to destroy the evidence of their bookmaking in a furnace. The burned papers were sent to the FBI Laboratory, and infrared photography of the charred scraps revealed handwritten names of race horses and figures listing betting odds (figure 1).

Ultraviolet photography of evidence in a California bank robbery furnished the first lead to the identification of the two criminals responsible. An aircraft employee's identification badge worn by one of the men was recovered near the scene of the robbery and submitted to the FBI Laboratory, where an examination disclosed that the original identification number on the badge had been removed and another number substituted. The cellophane cover of the badge was photographed by ultraviolet light, and the original identification number was revealed, leading directly to one of the bank robbers. Figure 2 shows the badge cover in ordinary light, and figure 3 the same cover in ultraviolet light.

A watermark whose design cannot be determined by ordinary photographic methods, because it is completely covered by handwriting, typewriting, or printing, can be photographed using "soft" X-rays, whose penetrating power is less than that of "hard" X-rays. This method will usually completely eliminate the written material, leaving on the photographic negative a picture of the watermark only. In a recent case involving the age of a questioned document, the usual methods of bringing out the watermark were of no value. However, soft X-rays completely dropped the printing, and the watermark was clearly shown. Figures 4 and 5 show a portion of the document photographed by transmitted light, and the same portion photographed by soft X-rays.

The many and varied types of examinations performed in the Document Section are to some extent

Figure 2

shown by the number of reference files maintained in this section. Some of these files against which evidence from law enforcement agencies is frequently checked include:

National Fraudulent Check File. --Photographs of fraudulent checks received in connection with cases previously examined in the Laboratory, with which current checks are compared.

Checkwriter Standards File. --Sample impressions of different styles of check protectors manufactured by various companies. Checkwriter impressions on fraudulent checks can be compared with this file to determine the kind of check protector used.

Safety Paper Standards File. --Samples of types of paper manufactured for use as check forms, including both designs for sale on the open market and special designs containing registered watermarks manufactured for a particular company or bank. The kind of paper used for a fictitious check form can be determined by means of this file.

Figure 3

Rubber Stamp and Printing Standards File. --Catalogs and samples of products made by rubber stamp and printing type manufacturers, for comparison with evidence bearing rubber stamp or printing type impressions.

Photocopier Standards File. --Samples of photocopies made using various office photocopy machines manufactured in the United States and some foreign countries. This file is of value in tracing photocopies to their original source.

Typewriter Standards File. --Samples of styles of type used on typewriters manufactured in the United States, as well as many of foreign manufacture. This file is of value not only in cases involving typewritten fraudulent checks, but for any kind of typewritten document.

Anonymous Letter File. --Photographs of extortion letters and other threatening communications received in connection with cases previously examined in the Laboratory, for comparison with current letters of this type.

Watermark File. --Photographs and brand names of watermarks and directories of paper manufacturers, to assist in determining the origin of paper containing a watermark.

National Motor Vehicle Certificate of Title File. --Samples of genuine state certificates of title and manufacturer's certificates of origin for comparison with documentary evidence submitted in automobile theft cases.

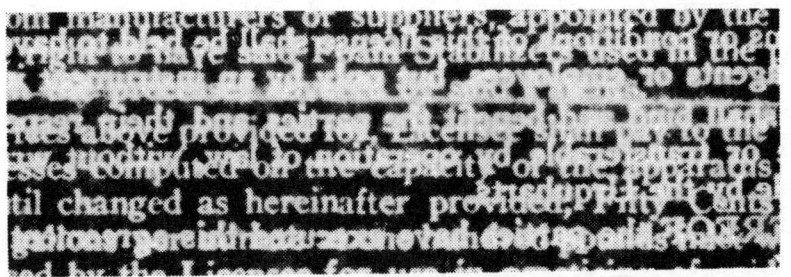

Figure 4

Much of the evidence received from law enforcement agencies for examination in the Document Section consists of bad checks. These checks range in value from 2 cents (a check given by an Army deserter as a "tip" to a waitress) to thousands of dollars. In skill of preparation they vary from crudely penciled scrawls to a group of beautifully hand-drawn and hand-lettered checks successfully passed by a man who prepared the entire check forms by hand with pen and ink on blank check paper (figure 6).

Since a considerable amount of the evidence received from law enforcement agencies consists of fraudulent checks, part of the discussion of documentary evidence in this article will be about such checks. The examinations of

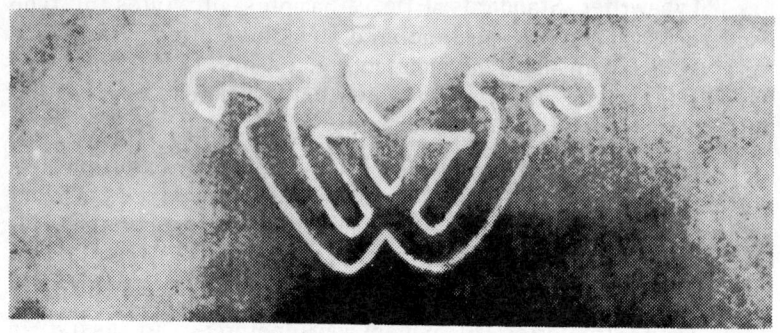

Figure 5

these checks cover a wide field--handwriting, typewriting, checkwriters, printing methods, safety papers, alterations, obliterations, and other factors.

This article will try to show the law enforcement officer what the FBI Laboratory can do to assist him, and what he can do to assist the Laboratory in making as thorough an examination of his evidence as possible.

Submission of Evidence

The letter to the FBI Laboratory covering the submission of checks or other evidence can be of much help to the document examiner if details concerning the crime are set out as fully as possible. The letter should be in duplicate, addressed to the Director, Federal Bureau of Investigation, Washington, D. C. 20535, marked for the attention of the FBI Laboratory, and if the evidence is sent under separate cover a copy of the letter should be with the evidence. A brief listing of the evidence should be given. If there has been previous correspondence in connection with the case, the last communication should be mentioned. The following points should be included in the letter, whenever possible.

1. Names of subject or suspect and victim, if known.
2. Nature of criminal violation.
3. Description of subject, real name (if known), and previous arrest record, if any.
4. Full description of circumstances surrounding the commission of the crime, including the modus operandi of the subject, any credentials used to pass checks, automobile (if one is used), other people with the subject, and any other

pertinent information. This point should be covered as fully as possible, as it may be of great value. For example, a recent check was identified with a group of previously submitted checks primarily on the basis of the modus operandi. The subject answered newspaper ads offering musical instruments (usually accordions) for sale by private individuals, gave these people bad checks for the instruments, then pawned them. In spite of the fact that the current check was signed with a name different from those on the previous checks, the document examiner recognized the modus operandi, and a positive identification was then made by means of a handwriting examination.

5. In the case of fraudulent checks, the letter to the FBI Laboratory should state whether the whole check was written in the presence of the victim or only endorsed in his presence, whether any part of the check (including all endorsements) was written by the victim or anyone else other than the suspect, whether any checks other than those submitted are known to have been passed by the suspect, whether any names on the checks are forgeries of a real person, whether the check form itself is stolen or fictitious, and, if a company name is used, whether this company is fictitious.

6. State whether the suspect, if known, is presently in custody.

When submitting any kind of evidence, the types of examinations desired should be set out, and a statement should be made as to whether the evidence may or may not be altered during the course of examination. Changes in the appearance

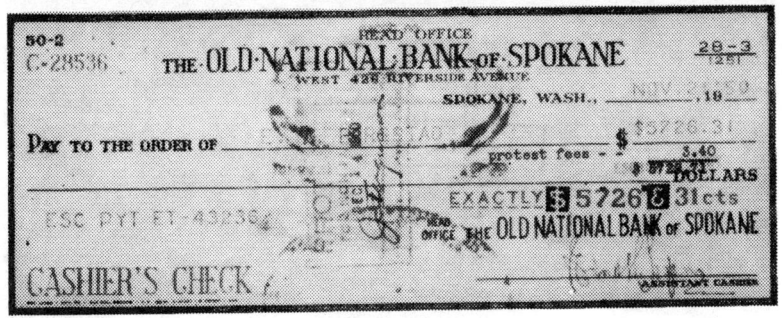

Figure 6

of evidence sometimes occur to some degree in certain examinations, such as in attempts to determine the approximate age of ink, or during chemical treatment to develop altered and obliterated writing or latent fingerprints. It is realized that these changes may sometimes be undesirable when such evidence may later be introduced in a trial. However, the law enforcement officer should weigh this possibility against the fact that chemical treatment may disclose information which can be invaluable in the investigation of a case, and which might otherwise go undetected. As a rule, chemical treatment changes the appearance of the evidence only slightly, and in no case is it completely destroyed. Also, photographs of the evidence in its original state are always made before any examination is conducted, and methods which will not alter the evidence are exhausted before any other treatment is attempted.

As an illustration of the importance of a complete examination of evidence, in a recent theft case several empty wooden crates were found by investigating officers in the possession of two suspects. The crates were the same size and shape as those which had contained the stolen items, but they were smeared with black paint, and there was nothing visible on them to show that they were the stolen crates. However, they were sent to the FBI Laboratory, where the paint was carefully removed, and underneath were found sten-

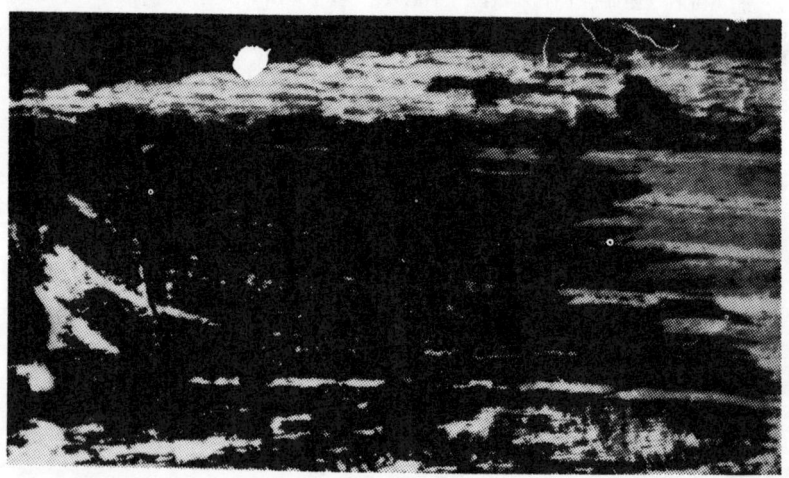

Figure 7

cilled letters and code numbers which definitely identified the crates as having once held the stolen property. Thus, the evidence was not returned to the investigating officers in the state in which it had been received by the Laboratory, but as proof of guilt the crates were of much more value in their altered state than they would have been otherwise. Figures 7 and 8 show a portion of one of the crates before and after treatment to remove the paint.

A statement should be included in the letter transmitting evidence that the evidence in the case has not been and will not be subjected to the same type of technical examination by any other expert.

Finally, the letter should indicate whether the evidence is to be returned to the contributor, or (as is usually the case when photographs of evidence are submitted) retained in the FBI Laboratory.

The Check Passer

Considering the millions of dollars realized each year by means of fraudulent checks, check-passing would seem to be a profitable "business" from the point of view of the passer. However, the money obtained from such activity generally proves to be hardly worth the time, trouble and anxiety involved, especially since the habitual check passer usually ends up in jail. One of the more active check

Figure 8

passers, recently rearrested after a short period of uneasy freedom, has spent a large part of the past 50 years in jail, yet the money he realized from his checks has hardly been enough for more than a moderate style of living.

In spite of these drawbacks, check-passing has a strong appeal for a certain type of person, who often prides himself on being among the "aristocracy" of the criminal world. The professional passer usually travels around the country stopping at one city just long enough to pass a check or two before moving on to the next city. It may be several days before the victim discovers that the check is bad, and by that time the passer may be hundreds of miles away, and the investigating officer has only a cold trail to follow. A typical example of this sort of operation is the case of a man recently apprehended in Missouri. He had stolen 150 blank company checks, and for 4 months had traveled from New York to California, cashing over $4,000 in bad checks. One of the first checks passed was sent to the FBI Laboratory, where it was identified with the signature on a fingerprint card in the files of the FBI's Identification Division, thus establishing the identity of the passer. After a chase which led halfway across the country, he was finally caught. He surrendered quietly, cheerfully admitted his guilt, and turned over to the arresting officers two publications he had been reading, Tales of Amazing Frauds and the Kefauver Crime Report.

The National Fraudulent Check File

Because of the widespread activity of fraudulent check passers, the FBI believed that a centralization of information about such criminals would be of assistance to investigating officers all over the country in their efforts to identify and locate these persons. Therefore, in 1936 the National Fraudulent Check File, a central reference collection of bad checks, was established as a part of the FBI Laboratory's Document Section. Representative photographs of checks in every case sent to the Laboratory for examination are added to this file, regardless of whether the case is a local matter or involves a Federal violation, and as current checks are received they are compared with material in this file.

When fraudulent checks are sent to the Laboratory, the signatures on these checks are first compared with similar names in the National Fraudulent Check File's collection of approximately 100,000 photographs of signatures used on checks previously submitted. If no identification is made in this manner, a search of other pertinent sections of the National Fraudulent Check File is made. By this method, nearly 50 percent of the checks submitted are identified as the work of persons who have passed checks previously examined by the Laboratory.

The value of the National Fraudulent check File is shown by a recent case in which 75 checks, involving over 30 different aliases, were tied together by means of this file. These checks had been submitted to the Laboratory by 35 different police departments and sheriffs' offices located in States all the way from Maine to California. Information regarding these checks was sent to all interested departments, along with the photograph and identification record of a suspect, thus furnishing valuable investigative leads which would not have been available without such a central file.

Examination of Checks

The primary purpose of the examination of a check is, as a rule, to attempt to identify the person responsible for its preparation. If such identity cannot be determined by means of the National Fraudulent Check File, many times an identification can be made through a comparison of the questioned signatures and endorsements on the check with signatures on fingerprint cards in the FBI's Identification Division of persons who have used similar names. In some cases, when a suspect has been located, a comparison of the questioned handwriting on the check with the known handwriting of the suspect is essential. Because of the limited nature of the handwriting on a check, which sometimes consists only of a signature, the proper obtaining of known handwriting specimens by the investigating officer is extremely important. Unless comparable specimens are submitted to the Laboratory, the document examiner may find it impossible to reach a definite conclusion either as to identity or nonidentity. The procedure for obtaining known specimens would be substantially as follows:

1. The suspect should not be allowed to see the questioned check before giving known handwriting specimens, in order to avoid the chance of influencing his manner of writing these specimens and to forestall any possible claim that he unconsciously copied the questioned handwriting.

2. Specimens should be written on blank check forms. If these are not immediately available, pieces of paper cut to the size of the questioned check and ruled with lines for writing corresponding to those on the fraudulent check may be used.

3. No instructions as to spelling, method of filling out the check forms, etc., should be given. The suspect should merely be told the date, payee, amount, signer and endorser (or any other questioned handwriting) on the check, and then be instructed to fill in the blank checks in a corresponding manner. This point is most important, as there are almost as many different ways of filling in checks as there are people who write them, and the professional check passer may develop habits in his manner of completing the various parts of a check which are often as characteristic as the handwriting itself. As an illustration of how the small sections of the whole check may be completed in distinctively different ways, figure 9 is a composit photograph of actual checks showing three out of many ways the "Dollars" line may be filed in.

4. The same type of writing instrument (nib pen, ballpoint pen, pencil, etc.) should be used to write the known specimens as that used for the questioned check, since the difference in writing quality between a smooth lead pencil point and a flexible broad nib pen, for example, may tend to influence certain characteristics in the handwriting. This point is especially important when the problem of disguise or forgery must be considered, because of the importance of line quality in such an examination.

5. As each check form is completed, it should be removed from the suspect's sight before the next one is written. In this connection, it is advisable to obtain numerous specimens in order to lessen the chance of attempted disguise, because the possibility of a suspect's being able consistently to alter his normal manner of writing decreases

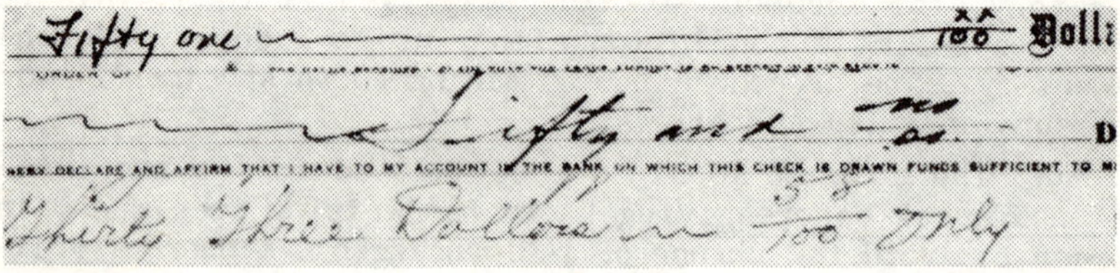

Figure 9

materially as he continues to write. Also, it is a good idea to obtain a few specimens written with the hand other than that normally used, especially if the questioned handwriting appears to be disguised.

6. If the known writing is of a different slant (forehand, vertical or backhand) or size from the questioned writing, the suspect should be instructed, *after* he has written several specimens without any instructions, to change the size or slant of his writing to correspond more nearly to that of the writing on the questioned check.

7. If any part of the check is handprinted, handprinting specimens should be obtained in both upper case and lower case handprinting in the exact wording of the questioned printing, since a comparison of handwriting with handprinting is for all practical purposes impossible.

8. For the purpose of introducing known specimens as evidence in court, the reverse side of each specimen should be dated and initialed by the witnessing officer, and a statement voluntarily given and signed by the suspect should be obtained to the effect that he has been advised of his constitutional rights, that the specimens are given freely and voluntarily and may be used against him in a court of law.

For the information of the document examiner, the letter to the FBI Laboratory transmitting known handwriting specimens should set out the manner of taking them and the instructions (if any) given to the suspect.

Other Specimens

If a suspect refuses to give handwriting specimens, any undictated known handwriting which can be located by the investigating officer may be of value. This undictated handwriting as a rule will not be as good for comparison purposes as dictated handwriting, because it will usually not contain wording similar to that on the questioned check, but if enough can be found containing certain letters and letter combinations in common with the questioned handwriting, it may be sufficient for a definite conclusion. School records, employment applications, automobile registrations, legitimate checks, personal letters, various types of business papers, etc., are possible sources of undictated handwriting. The more of such handwriting the document examiner has at his disposal, the better are the chances of his reaching a conclusion. When locating these specimens, the investigating officer should keep in mind the problem of proving the authenticity of such handwriting in court.

The identification of the handwriting on a check with the known handwriting of a suspect is, of course, of great value in the prosecution of a case, and such testimony by an expert document examiner in court is frequently enough to convince a jury of the subject's guilt. For this reason, the possibility of a handwriting identification should be kept in mind even if the investigation of a case is an extended one. For example, in one case a payroll check of an Arkansas mining company was stolen from an employee of the company, endorsed by the thief, and cashed. For 3 years investigation continued, and a suspect was finally developed. However, he refused to admit his guilt, counting on the long lapse of time since the passing of the check to protect him. Numerous known specimens of his method of writing the questioned endorsement were submitted to the Laboratory, and, in spite of the 3 years between the writings, a positive identification was made. When confronted with the results of this handwriting examination, the suspect admitted his guilt. Figure 10 shows the questioned endorsement, and figure 11 shows one of the known signatures written 3 years later.

Figure 10

Figure 11

The value of handwriting examinations in eliminating as well as identifying suspects should also be considered during the course of an investigation. Sometimes such an examination will even disclose evidence seemingly contrary to facts, but which later proves to be true. Such a case occurred some time ago in the Midwest, where in a State court a man was convicted of passing bad checks on the testimony of five "eye witnesses" who identified the man as the person passing the checks. However, a document examination of the checks by the FBI Laboratory showed that he could not have written them. Additional investigation established the fact that the convicted man was actually in another State on the day the checks were passed. The Governor of the State in which the man was convicted, upon learning of these facts, granted a full pardon.

Forgery of Genuine Signature

The question of forgery of a genuine signature may sometimes enter into a fraudulent check investigation. A recent case began with the marriage of a 40-year-old woman to her fifth husband, 82 years old and wealthy. Two days after they married she disappeared, along with $11,500 in bank drafts and checks belonging to her husband. He swore out a warrant, and a few days later she was located and arrested. She insisted that he had given her the checks, but when they were found in a Florida bank where she had cashed them, they were sent to the FBI Laboratory, and an examination revealed that his signatures on the checks had been traced directly from one of his genuine signatures. The woman was convicted and given a sentence of 5 years. Figure 12 is a photograph of one of the questioned forgeries, and figure 13 is the known signature.

Figure 12

Figure 13

In this particular case the forgeries were proved not

only by the fact that all the usual signs of forgery (uneven line quality, wavering strokes, etc.) were present, but also by the fact that the questioned signatures could be directly superimposed over the known signature. This proved conclusively that they were *traced* forgeries, and this conclusion was later supported by a statement from the woman's son that he had seen her place the questioned checks over the genuine signature on top of a strong light and trace the signatures directly on the checks. Because of the complicated and varied movements made by the hand in writing such a habitual thing as a signature, it is impossible to duplicate these movements exactly. Therefore, no two genuine signatures can be directly superimposed even though the basic handwriting characteristics themselves are constant.

Even when the particular known signature from which a questioned forgery was traced cannot be located, evidence of this type of forgery may still be shown by a document examination. Microscopic examinations and infrared photography may reveal unnatural indentations along the lines of writing, or faint pencil lines or deposits from carbon paper under the ink lines, all of which may be indications of a traced forgery.

Another type of forgery is the *copied* forgery, a more-or-less "free-hand" simulation of a genuine signature. When comparing a copied forgery with a known signature it is usually possible by means of a microscopic examination of line quality, flow of ink, smoothness of writing, retouching of lines, breaks in the writing, retracing of lines and other factors, to show that the questioned signature is actually a forgery--that is, an imitation of the true signature. However, as is also true of a traced forgery, since it is an imitation it may not contain sufficient normal handwriting characteristics of the actual writer to enable it to be identified as the work of a particular person. For this reason, when submitting suspected forged signatures to the Laboratory for examination, the investigating officer should also submit genuine signatures of the person whose signature was forged.

The names and signatures appearing in this article are shown only because they are among those which have at some time been forged or used as aliases by check passers. No unfavorable reference is intended to any person using any of these names legitimately.

Mechanically Made Checks

Many professional check passers, depending on their own ability at putting up a good "front" to cheat their victims, write their checks entirely by hand and use regular check forms. However, through the efforts of law enforcement agencies and other interested organizations, the public is increasingly being made aware of the possibility of being defrauded by accepting bad checks. The check passer is thus forced to attempt to create more elaborate checks, as genuine in appearance as possible. Therefore he often turns to mechanical aids for producing his checks.

Laboratory examinations of these mechanically made checks frequently involve problems and techniques entirely different from those involved in the examination of a handwritten check. In order to perform as thorough an examination of this type of check as possible, the Document Section maintains (in addition to the National Fraudulent Check File) the Checkwriter Standards File, Safety Paper Standards File, Rubber Stamp and Printing Standards File and Typewriter Standards File. These known standards have proved their usefulness many times in connection with checks and other types of evidence examined in the Document Section. For example, the value of the Safety Paper Standards File can be shown by a case in which the use of this file led directly to the apprehension of a man who had successfully passed over 250 checks amounting to thousands of dollars. At first he used bank checks and similar types of check forms which could easily be obtained by anyone. However, he later began to use fictitious company checks, printed on a certain type of safety paper. Investigating officers were able to trace this particular design of paper from the manufacturer to the retailer, and then to a print shop. The printer stated that he had printed 1,500 checks, similar to the questioned checks, for a man whom he expected to return soon for another order. A surveillance was placed on the print shop and the suspect was apprehended. Later a positive identification of his handwriting with the handwriting on the questioned checks was made. He pleaded guilty and received a 5-year sentence.

Another case handled in the Document Section illustrates the use of printing standards in the examination of type faces on fraudulent checks. This case concerned an ex-convict and printer who used his employer's print shop equipment after hours to make fraudulent check forms. Within a few months he passed over 100 checks in the Southwest, using a dozen different aliases. However, this habit of using various names eventually led to his downfall. He absentmindedly endorsed one check with a name other than that of the payee on the check, realized his mistake too late, grabbed the check and tried to escape, but was caught. The many different styles of printing type used on the questioned checks were examined in the Document Section, and all were identified as styles manufactured by the same company. In addition, microscopic defects in the type faces themselves turned up again and again on the checks. The "check protector" impressions on the checks were a most unusual and individual characteristic too. No actual check protector was used, but metal type faces were carefully scarified with a file, and then printed directly on the checks to simulate a real check protector. The subject of this case was convicted and sentenced to a term of 15 years. Figure 14 is a photograph of one of these checks, showing the various styles of type faces and the "check protector" impressions.

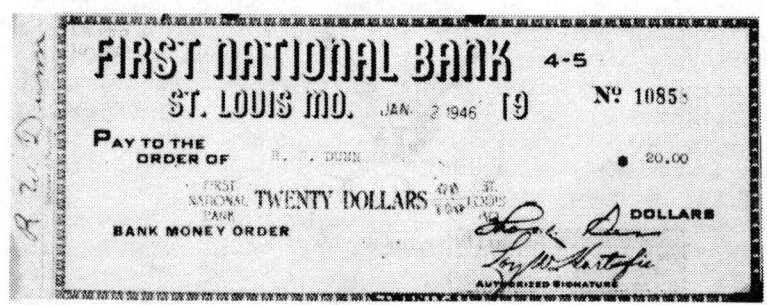

Figure 14

Because the handwriting on a check filled out by means of a check protector, typewriter or other mechanical means may be extremely limited or disguised, often consisting only of a signature or endorsement, a positive identification with known handwriting of a suspect may be difficult, if not impossible, and other means of identification must be sought. If a suspect has in his possession material such as check protectors, typewriters, rubber stamps or similar devices, known specimens of those items should be submitted for examination, together with the questioned checks, since such examinations may often furnish positive proof of the

Figure 15

suspect's connection with the fraudulent checks. One of the most extensive check cases ever handled by the FBI Laboratory's Document Section involved the examination of almost 400 checks passed in 28 States by a man who boasted after his apprehension that he had cashed $100,000 in bad checks within 18 months. In spite of the varied appearance of these checks, they were all eventually identified as the work of this man, partly by examination of his handwriting and partly by examination of the equipment found in his possession at the time of his arrest. This equipment included rubber stamp sets, fountain pens, a check protector, two typewriters, a printing press, trays of metal type, and tubes of printers' inks. Figure 15 shows some of this equipment.

Obtaining Known Specimens

Because the questioned material on a fraudulent check is usually quite limited, the investigating officer should take special care to obtain adequate and comparable known specimens. When a check protector or typewriter belonging to a suspect has been located, it is not necessary to send in the machine itself, but numerous known specimens should be made. These should be in the exact wording or numbering of the questioned material and, if possible, should be made on paper similar in thickness and finish to the paper used for the questioned checks. A few specimens showing all of the letters and characters on the machine should also be made, for use in possible future comparisons.

When a known typewriter is located certain other steps may be taken in addition to the above instructions. When making known specimens on a typewriter, two methods should be used. The first is the usual method of typing directly on paper through the typewriter ribbon. The second method involves the taking of so-called "carbon" specimens. These are made by laying a sheet of carbon paper over a sheet of bond paper, setting the machine on stencil (or removing the ribbon), and typing directly on the carbon paper. This method produces clear-cut impressions of the type faces, which impressions are almost as valuable in a comparison as the actual type faces themselves since there is no distortion or indistinct outline such as is sometimes caused by typing through a ribbon. If the typewriter ribbon appears to be fairly new, or has not been used very much, this ribbon may be removed from the machine and sent to the FBI Laboratory. It will then be examined to see if impressions of the questioned typewriting on the check can be found on the ribbon. Of course, if the original ribbon is to be submitted to the FBI Laboratory for examination, it should be removed from the typewriter and another ribbon used for the taking of the known specimens.

When making known specimens on a typewriter, some samples using light, medium and heavy touches should be made, since the appearance of a typewritten character may be changed slightly as the touch varies.

All specimens made on check protectors and typewriters should be dated and initialed by the person taking the specimens. The make, model and serial number of the machine should also be noted.

Rubber Stamps

Rubber stamps are frequently used on fraudulent checks, as in the preparation of dates, fictitious company names, bank certifications, cashiers' stamps or other material. These rubber stamp impressions may contain individual characteristics which can be definitely identified with a known stamp. Such characteristics may be caused by usage, accidental cuts, defects in the original type used to make the stamp, and dirt or other foreign matter on the stamp. Stamps made of individual letters of rubber type (such as those in toy stamp sets) are set by hand, and are often unevenly aligned. These irregularities in alignment can be most significant in a comparison with a questioned stamp impression.

In order to determine the significance of certain characteristics present in a questioned rubber stamp impression, an examination of the known rubber stamp itself is highly advisable. Therefore the stamps themselves, rather than known impressions made from them, should be sent to the FBI Laboratory for examination whenever possible. The surfaces of these stamps should not be cleaned or otherwise disturbed, and extreme care should be taken in packing them so that any foreign matter, or in case of a handset stamp the positions of the individual letters themselves, will not be disturbed. The initials of the investigating officer and the date should be scratched on the wooden portion of the stamp for possible introduction as evidence in court.

When comparisons of fraudulent checks with known specimens of check protectors, typewriters, rubber stamps or similar items are requested, the original questioned checks, rather than photographs or photostats, should be submitted whenever possible. The characteristics on which identifications of such material are made are often microscopic in nature, and an examination of the original checks is advisable in order properly to evaluate these characteristics.

In addition to the more usual types of examinations of fraudulent checks, other examinations which are more or less individual with each check may sometimes be necessary. Such examinations may involve obliterations, alterations, line crossings, torn paper or other unusual factors, and, almost without exception, require that the original check rather than a copy be made available for examination.

Obliterations and alterations may be found in various types of check cases, such as those in which a genuine check is stolen and erasures or changes are made on the check by the thief in order that he might cash it or raise the amount of the check. The methods of developing obliterated material or uncovering alterations vary with the individual case, depending on the way in which the original material was prepared and the way it was changed. Erased pencil writing may be made visible by photographing with infrared light (if traces of graphite are still present), or the indentations made in the paper by the pencil point may be shown by photographing with parallel light rays or (if the indentations are shallow) by treating with iodine fumes. However, the success of the iodine fuming method depends to a great extent on the composition of the paper and the amount of fiber disturbance caused by the writing. If pencil writing has been covered over with ink, the original writing may be revealed by photographing with infrared light or by chemical treatment. Ink writing which has been obliterated with a covering material or bleached may be made visible by photographing with infrared or ultraviolet light or restored by chemical treatment. Indentations made by a stiff pen nib (such as a ball-point pen) may be examined in the same manner as those made by a pencil. In addition to these methods, microscopic examination of any remaining fragments of the original material or photography with different types of color filters may also be of value in the examination of obliterations and alterations.

The investigating officer, when submitting checks suspected of having been altered, should bear in mind the fact that although microscopic and photographic examinations will not change the original appearance of this evidence, chemical treatment will change it to some extent. Therefore, the letter transmitting the evidence should state specifically whether tests which may change its appearance may or may not be performed by the FBI Laboratory. In this regard, it is pointed out that although such changes may sometimes not be desirable from a legal point of view, they may be directly responsible for the solution of the case. Photographs of documentary evidence as it was originally received in the FBI Laboratory are always made before any tests are performed.

An unusual case involving an obliteration occurred a few years ago when a woman was arrested in Ohio for issuing to a store a check which was returned by the bank marked "No Account." However, she claimed that when she gave the check to the store clerk she wrote on it that it was to be held until she made payment at the store. No such notation was visible on the check, and it was sent to the FBI Laboratory. There, microscopic examination showed paper fiber disturbances and slight traces of stains on one corner of the check. This portion was photographed under ultraviolet light, and the handwritten words "hold this till I Pay" were then clearly visible. The case against the woman was dismissed. Figure 16 shows a portion of this check photographed with ordinary light, and figure 17 is the same portion photographed under ultraviolet light.

Figure 16

Figure 17

Another check case examined in the Document Section furnished an illustration of a torn paper examination. This case concerned a man whose career as a forger began when he was 15 years old and lasted 40 years, more than half of which time was spent in jail. During his 1½ years of freedom before his latest arrest, he traveled all over the United States, using over 100 aliases, and passed checks totaling $96,000. As these checks came into the Laboratory, they were all recognized as the work of this check artist. When he was finally apprehended, the equipment found in his possession was sent to the Document Section for examination. In addition to the identification of his handwriting on the checks, rubber stamps and a typewriter were identified with material on some of the checks. Checkbooks of several different banks were also found in his possession, and the serrated edges of many of the fraudulent checks were found to match perfectly the edges of some of the check stubs in these books. Figure 18 shows a portion of one of the checks matched with the check stub from which it was torn.

One of the most interesting cases of check-raising, and a good example of the comprehensive examinations which sometimes must be made of a check, occurred several years ago in

Ohio. A check for $200 given by a man to an acquaintance grew into a check for $6,200 by the time it was cashed. This check was sent to the Laboratory, and examination under a microscope showed definite disturbances of the paper fibers, indicating erasures in the amount. Infrared photography revealed traces of the erased word "Two" under the words "Sixty-two." Color filter photography showed that the ink writing on the entire check had been retouched in an effort to conceal the slight difference in color of the ink used to write the words "Sixty-two" and the figure "6" in front of the original figures "200.00." Microscopic photography disclosed that the cross bar on the "T" in "Two" was on top of the first stroke of the "H" in "Hundred," indicating that the words "Sixty-two" had been written *after* the word "Hundred." A handwriting examination proved that the man who had originally made out the check had not written the words "Sixty-two." All of this evidence was more than enough to

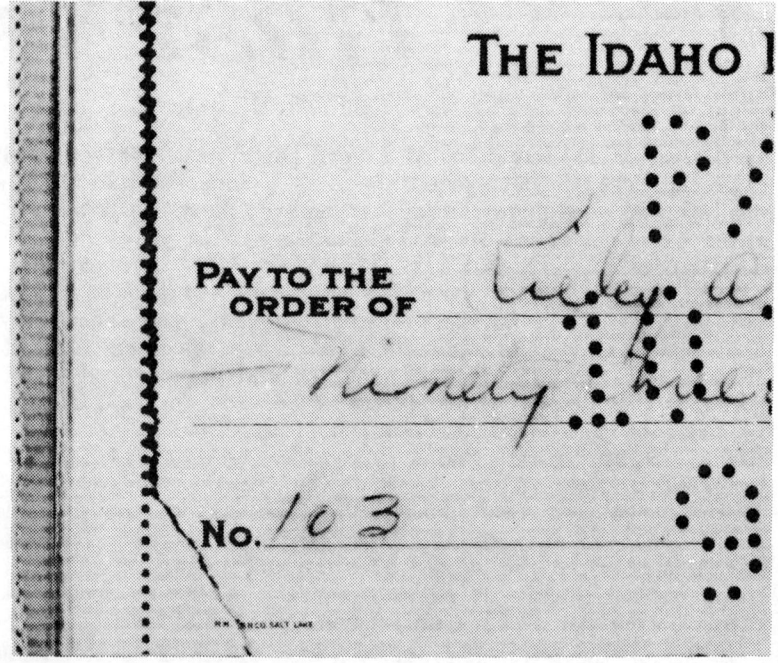

Figure 18

Figure 19

convince a jury of the defendant's guilt. Figure 19 is a photograph of the entire check made with a color filter. Note (especially in the signature) the light lines of the original writing and the darker lines of the retouching.

With respect to line crossings, which played an important part in this examination, the determination of which of two lines is on top may in certain situations be of invaluable aid to the investigator by showing the sequence of writing or by proving or disproving the authenticity of a document. Because of the many factors which must be considered, such as the age of the writing, the type of writing instrument (pen, pencil, typewriter, etc.), the kind of paper and the storage conditions of the document, the results of such an examination may not always be conclusive, but information of value can sometimes be brought to light.

Documentary Evidence

This article has previously discussed the submission of evidence to the Laboratory, the obtaining of known specimens and the various types of examinations which could be made in fraudulent check cases. However, many of the techniques used in the examination of checks are equally applicable to documentary evidence which may appear in dozens of other types of criminal violations. In all these cases--extortions, robberies, kidnappings, murders and many others, as well as the less sensational check cases--the document examiner uses his technical skill and scientific knowledge to uncover by impartial examination of a questioned document every fact which may help to bring an investigation to an equitable conclusion.

Submission of Evidence

In certain types of cases the presence of evidence which lends itself to a document examination may not be as obvious as in cases such as those involving fraudulent checks or anonymous letters. However, the law enforcement officer should keep in mind during all his investigations that almost any type of evidence, even the most unlikely appearing, may be susceptible to some sort of laboratory examination and may disclose an unexpected fact without which the solution of the case would be extremely difficult or even impossible. For example, a burnt paper match--a seemingly trivial bit of evidence which could easily have been overlooked was picked up at the scene of a crime and was later shown to have been torn from a folder of paper matches found in the possession of a suspect. Figure 20 is an enlarged photograph of part of the matchbook, showing how the irregular tear at the base of the burnt match fitted the stub still remaining in the folder.

The method of submission of checks and other documentary evidence to the FBI Laboratory was discussed previously in this article and only a few additional points applying to certain types of evidence need be mentioned. Documentary evidence requiring a latent fingerprint examination should be placed in a suitable container such as a cellophane envelope or a paper envelope which can be sealed. Charred paper should be loosely packed between layers of cotton in a

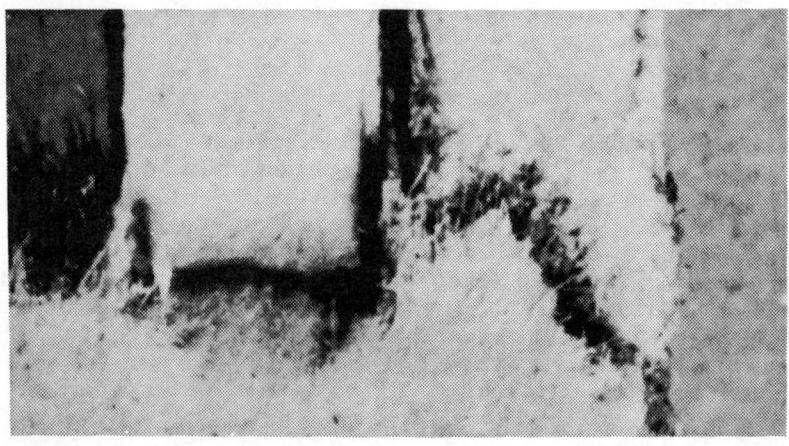

Figure 20

strong rigid container, and should not be moistened or flattened. Paper bearing indented writing, or evidence bearing questioned features which might be altered by friction or wear, should not be folded and should be packed so as to avoid heavy pressure or rubbing

Types of Examinations

Document examinations generally fall into certain broad classifications, such as examinations of paper, writing instruments, handwriting, obliterations and alterations, or other primary groups. However, it is almost impossible to set out specifically all of the kinds of documentary examinations which can be made, or what may be disclosed through such examinations, because each piece of evidence may often present its own individual problems. Therefore, when making an examination the document examiner considers not only the obvious aspects of the evidence, but also looks for the more obscure factors which may be highly important in determining its significance.

Examinations of paper or paper products are made in order to determine the original source or manufacturer of the paper, to prove or disprove the genuineness of a document, to connect a questioned piece of evidence directly with known evidence, or for other purposes. These determinations may be made in many ways, depending on the character of the evidence itself. A watermark in paper is one of the best methods of tracing the manufacturer, since watermarks are registered with the United States Patent Office by companies which manufacture paper or use watermarks for identification. The Document Section's Watermark File, which contains photographs and brand names of watermarks, is a valuable source of information for determining the origin of paper containing a watermark.

If the date of a document containing a watermark is in question, this watermark may indicate when the paper was manufactured, thus tending to prove or disprove the document's authenticity. Occasionally the year of manufacture may be incorporated into the design of the watermark itself, or changes in the design of a particular watermark may give a clue as to the date of its use. However, a watermark is only one way of determining the authenticity of a document through its date. Other ways may involve examinations such as typewriting or printing-type comparisons. Examinations of inks or paper sizing and fibers may also furnish leads, but these examinations are usually not conclusive. Inks may be affected by storage conditions of the document, the temperature and humidity to which it was exposed, and other variable factors. Paper sizing and fibers have become so standardized among paper manufacturers over the past several decades that positive determinations are not often possible unless the span of time in question is very wide.

As an example of the use of a typewriting examination in uncovering a fraud, a West Virginia law enforcement agency sent to the FBI Laboratory some deeds which had been purportedly admitted to record in 1910, 1913, and 1918. It was determined that all of these deeds were typed on the same machine, and when the style of type was compared with the Document Section's Typewriter Standards File it was discovered that this particular style of type was not in use until 1927.

Another case illustrating the possibilities of determining the genuineness of a document by its date occurred during World War II, when a Selective Service Board in an Alabama town learned that the sons of a local farmer had not registered. The parents contended that the boys were too young to register and produced delayed birth certificates issued solely on the basis of records in a "family Bible" to show that their sons were born in 1928 and 1930. Examination of this Bible by the FBI Laboratory showed that it had been artificially aged and that the license to print this particular Bible was not issued until 1939, thereby completely disproving the parents' claim that their sons' birth dates had been written in this Bible a few days after the births in 1928 and 1930.

An attempted fraud which was exposed by an examination in the Document Section concerned a document purportedly written almost 200 years ago. However, analysis of the paper fibers disclosed the presence of chemical wood pulp, which was not used prior to the middle of the nineteenth century. Furthermore, the ink writing on the note was still a fresh blue color, quite different from the faded yellowish-brown it should have been, and the pen nib marks were of the type made by a fountain pen or a steel pen, not the quill pen of the eighteenth century.

Physical Characteristics

Examination of the physical characteristics and chemical composition of paper evidence may furnish investigative leads as to its original source, may prove valuable in comparisons with known evidence, or may uncover other facts pertinent to the case under investigation. However, unless otherwise authorized by the contributor, the FBI Laboratory makes only such examinations as will not change the original appearance of the evidence. Most of the chemical tests, and a few of the physical tests, will change the evidence to varying degrees, but many tests can be made which will not. These include determinations of dimensions, weight, texture and color; microscopic, spectrophotometric, ultraviolet and soft X-ray examinations, and others. Such examinations as determination of fiber content, sizing tests, artificial aging tests or spectrographic examination will alter the evidence or destroy small portions of it.

In addition to the properties of paper evidence which are inherent in the paper itself, there are the more-or-less "accidental" properties--tears or cuts, stains, serrated edges (such as those on postage stamps or checks and check stubs), irregular nicks caused by the manufacturer's paper cutting knife, and many other individual peculiarities which are extremely valuable in a comparison with known evidence. As an illustration of the possibilities of such individual characteristics, a California bank was robbed by a man who

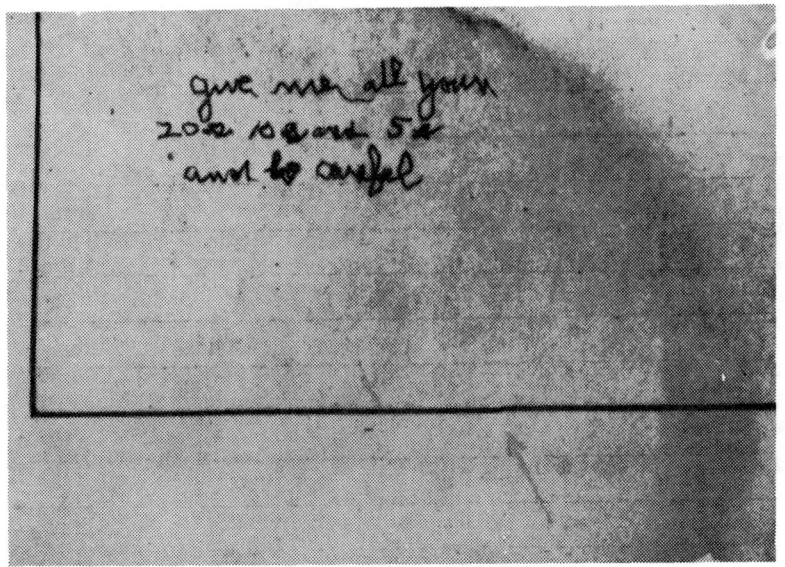

Figure 21

handed the teller a note reading "give me all your 20's, 10's, and 5's and be careful." A suspect was arrested, and in his home was found a notebook containing paper similar to the demand note. This notebook, the robbery note and samples of his handwriting were sent to the FBI Laboratory. An examination showed not only that the suspect had written the note, but that the paper on which it was written had been cut from a page still in his notebook. This was proved by the fact that the two cut edges of the note matched in microscopic detail with the cut edges of the remainder of the page, and that a portion of a stain on the note matched the remainder of the stain on the page. Figure 21 is a reduced reproduction of the note and a portion of the remainder of the notebook page (separated by a black line), showing the matching of the two cut edges and the dark stain.

The examination of serrated or notched edges has previously been mentioned in identifying a fraudulent check with a checkbook stub from which it was torn. This type of examination may also be necessary for other types of evidence, such as postage stamps, "saw-toothed" paper bags or wax paper torn on a notched metal edge. As a rule, the examination of serrations is necessarily microscopic in nature, and extreme care should be taken in handling such evidence in order that the edges may be disturbed as little as possible.

As an illustration of a postage stamp examination, a threatening letter was received by a man in Alabama. A suspect was apprehended, and specimens of his handwriting, along with stationery and postage stamps found in his possession, were sent to the FBI Laboratory. In addition to identifications of the handwriting and stationery, the strip of three stamps on the envelope was proved by a comparison of the serrated edges to have been originally connected to the stamps found in the suspect's possession. As further proof, special photography showed that both the known and questioned stamps had come from the same vending machine, as revealed by the indentations on the stamps caused by the machine.

The matching of torn or cut edges (such as those illustrated by figures 21 and 22), like the matching of serrated edges, requires an examination which is primarily microscopic. This type of examination often proves to be extremely valuable, not only in identifying questioned evidence with known, but in other situations as well. For example, in a case involving several documents sealed with cellophane

tape, the sequence of the sealing of the documents became
important. By examining the torn ends of each piece of tape
it was possible to match them, one after the other, thus
showing the exact order in which each piece had been torn
from the roll of tape. Figure 22 is a photomicrograph of
portions of two strips of tape, showing the matching ends.

Various types of examinations of the inherent and accidental properties of paper evidence, in addition to the more
usual one described above, are often necessary. As stated
previously, it is almost impossible to describe all the possibilities which may arise in examining paper evidence,
since the type of examination often depends on the individual evidence itself. However, two cases may serve as examples of the type of situation the document examiner often
faces. One case concerned a man suspected of arson in the
burning of a store in North Carolina. Several paper bags
found at the scene of the fire were sent to the FBI Labora-

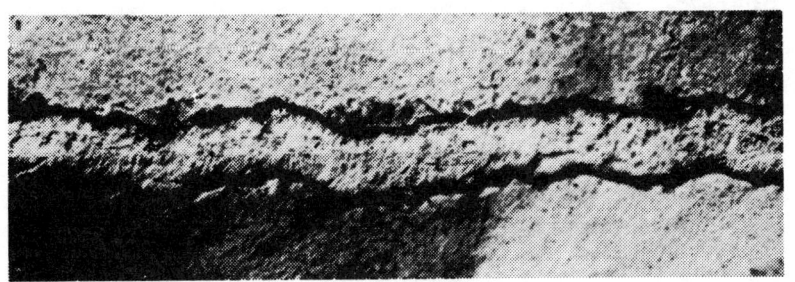

Figure 22

tory, along with some paper bags found in the suspect's car.
The known and questioned bags were found to be similar in
every respect--physical characteristics, edges, foldings and
other features. In addition, it was possible to prove by an
examination of certain individual peculiarities that all of
the bags had actually been made on the same machine.

The second case involved a Colorado woman who had been
receiving threatening letters from a former suitor. However, only one of the letters had been postmarked. When the
man was interviewed, he admitted writing this letter but
denied mailing it. He claimed that he had personally placed
it in the woman's mailbox, and that she had then put it in
an envelope in which he had previously mailed an innocuous
letter to her, in order to frame him on a Federal charge.

Figure 23

The questioned letter and envelope were sent to the FBI Laboratory to attempt to determine whether the letter had actually been mailed in the envelope. An examination revealed that some of the glue on the flap of the envelope had stuck to the letter in such a manner that when the envelope was opened some of the paper fibers from the letter were torn off and adhered to the envelope flap. In addition, other portions of the glue on the flap adhered to the letter. Thus, it was possible to state definitely that the threatening letter was in the envelope at the time it was sealed. Figure 23 is a photograph of portions of the envelope (lower) and letter (upper), showing how the spots of glue match. Figure 24 is an enlarged photograph of portions of the envelope and letter, showing how the paper fibers adhering to the flap match the torn portions of the letter.

Concealed Clues

The performance of a criminal act is often a deliberate gamble on the part of the criminal, based on his erroneous belief that he is a little smarter than the law-enforcement investigator. However, one thing he fails to take into account is his own ignorance of the extent to which scientific examination of evidence may be carried by the modern laboratory.

The criminal may attempt to disguise his handwriting, or carefully avoid leaving his fingerprints on a document, yet other equally incriminating evidence may completely escape his notice or be beyond his control. Some of these less obvious features of documentary evidence (which were discussed previously in this article) include such factors as the inherent properties of paper, which may contradict

Figure 24

the impression the criminal is trying to create, or accidental markings, such as tears, cuts or stains, of which he may not be aware.

In addition to the inherent and accidental properties of documentary evidence, there are other types of features, such as idented writing or transferred writing, which are produced by the criminal as a direct result of his original writing, and which may be completely unnoticed by him. Also, sometimes there may be incriminating aspects of a document of which the criminal is perfectly aware, and which he therefore attempts to destroy. These attempts reach the laboratory in the form of erasures, obliterations, burned paper or other forms. However, although the deliberate destruction of evidence by erasing, obliterating or burning may seem successful to the criminal, a laboratory examination will often uncover the very things he so carefully, even laboriously, attempts to conceal.

Indented Writing

When the top sheet of a stack of two or more sheets of paper is written on, the pressure of the writing instrument may be sufficient to cause slight depressions or indentations in one or more sheets of paper immediately beneath the top one. With proper examination these indentations, usually illegible under ordinary conditions, may be made readable. Indentations may also be made by a typewriter, as when a sheet of paper is used as a backing under the top sheet in order to avoid excessive wear on the platen. Indentations caused by printing type may also occasionally be found.

Indented writing is first examined visually and photographed with a strong light shining across the paper, almost parallel to its surface. This tends to emphasize the indentations in the paper, much as the headlights of an automobile show up the hollows in a road at night. If visual examination of the paper and study of the photographs prove unsatisfactory, other methods such as iodine fuming or chemical treatment may be used.

Because indented writing is not readily visible under ordinary lighting conditions, paper containing such writing may be overlooked during the search of a crime scene. However, the beam of a flashlight held across a suspected piece of paper may be sufficient to indicate the presence of indentations.

As an example of the value of indented writing, the solving of the murder of a New York patrolman came about largely as the result of such an examination. The patrolman stopped a stolen car, placed the two men in it under arrest, and wrote their names and addresses in his logbook. However, one of the men drew a gun and killed the patrolman, then tore the incriminating page from the logbook and both men fled the scene. The book was sent to the FBI Laboratory for examination of the blank pages, for possible indented writing, and two names and an address were found. The names proved to be fictitious, but continuing investigation in the neighborhood of the address located the two men living only a few doors away from the number they had given as their

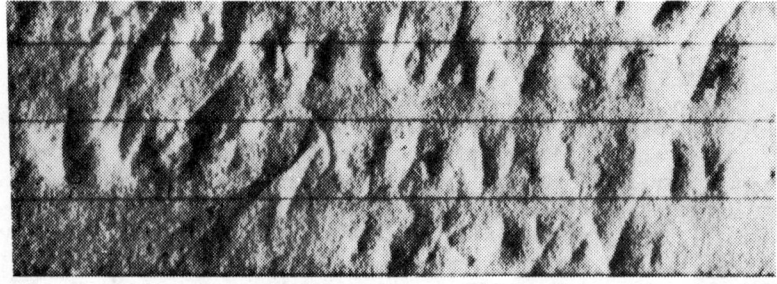

Figure 25

address. Figure 25 is a portion of the logbook page showing the indented writing.

Indented writing also figured in one of the most sensational kidnapings of recent years, the abduction of a 9-year-old girl in New Mexico. A woman doctor was apprehended at the payoff scene, and, in addition to other evidence, a tablet found in her home bore indentations which perfectly matched the handprinting on one of the ransom notes found in her possession.

Transferred Writing

Transferred writing, like indented writing, is a byproduct of the original and visible writing, and may often go unnoticed or unheeded by the criminal. The "mirror image" left on a blotter when ink writing is blotted is a simple example of transferred writing. Transfers may also occur under other conditions, such as when a sheet of paper is laid over another sheet bearing still-wet ink writing. An interesting type of transfer, the possibility of which should be considered if the sequence of writing of two or more pages of pencil writing is questioned, is the transfer of faint portions (usually microscopic in nature) of the pencil lines from one sheet to the back of a sheet directly above it, caused by the pressure of the writing instrument on the top sheet.

Under certain conditions, graphite or carbon traces from pencil or carbon writing may be transferred from one piece of paper to another when the two papers are in close contact for some time and are subject to a certain amount of pressure or friction (as, for example, papers carried in the pocket or in a wallet). These transfers are mirror images

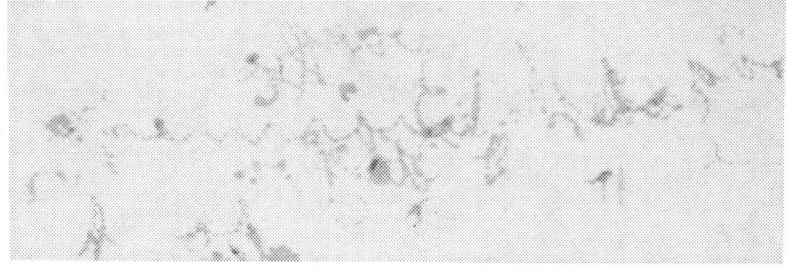

Figure 26

and are usually quite faint, but may become legible through
special photographic methods. Still another type of transfer which may occasionally occur is caused by the tendency
of certain invisible components of some inks to transfer to
a sheet of paper which has been in direct contact with the
ink writing for a long time. Under proper chemical treatment, or by means of special photography, this transferred
material may sometimes be made visible.

The conviction of an income-tax evader in New York was
brought about primarily because of proof supported by an examination of transferred graphite deposits from pencil writing. The defendant claimed he had written a letter to the
Collector of Internal Revenue (which the collector never received) offering voluntary disclosure, and stated that this
letter had been written before the start of the Internal
Revenue investigation. As proof, he offered his stenographer's notebook containing penciled shorthand notes of the
letter dated before the investigation. The notebook was
sent to the FBI Laboratory for examination to see if the
notes were as old as they purported to be. Because of the
short span of time in question and the fact that pencil
writing is chemically inert, no chemical treatment was feasible. However, microscopic examination of the reverse side
of the notebook page containing the questioned letter revealed traces of graphite which had been directly transferred by the pressure of the point of the writing instrument from penciled notes on the page underneath--notes dated
several weeks later than the questioned letter--which traces
could not possibly have occurred unless the notes bearing
the later date had actually been there first.

A bank robbery in Iowa furnishes another instance of
the value of transferred writing. The robber handed the

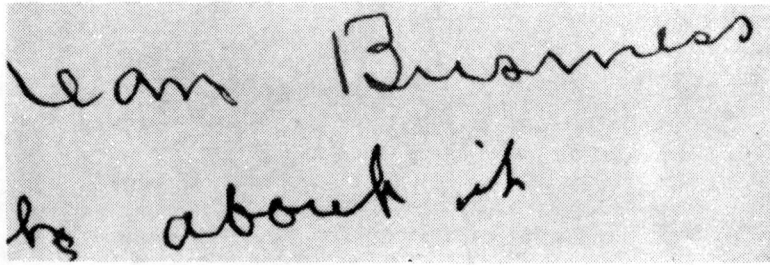

Figure 27

teller a threatening note written in ink and escaped with
$20,000. A blotter found in a hotel room was thought to
contain part of the wording of the note, and upon examination the words were proved to have been transferred directly
from the ink writing on the note itself. The occupant of
the room had checked out, but was located in California. A
comparison of his handwriting with the handwriting on the
note showed significant characteristics in common, and he
was tried and convicted for the robbery. Figure 26 is a
portion of the blotter showing, among other fragments transferred from the note, the word "Business." Figure 27 is the
portion of the note containing this word.

Alterations and Obliterations

The methods of detecting alterations and obliterations
or erasures on documents, and the possibility of interpreting the original material, depend to a great extent on the
type of paper used, the medium of writing, and the method
used to obliterate or alter. The original writing, which
could be concealed or partially destroyed by any one of many
ways, may range from light pencil writing to heavy printing
ink, and the surface on which it originally appeared may be
anything from a good grade of smooth bond paper to a rough
cheap cardboard--or material such as leather or wood.

Obliterations and alterations were discussed to some
extent previously in this article in connection with fraudulent checks, and the same methods of detection and treatment
apply equally well to other types of evidence. Microscopic
examination of the suspected area of a document under strong
side-lighting often uncovers evidences of erasures or eradications on paper, no matter how skillfully done, because of the almost inevitable fiber disturbance or change in the surface appearance of the paper.

Figure 28

This side-lighting may also reveal
identations left by the original writing which can then be
examined in the same manner as ordinary indented writing.

If microscopic or visual examination produces inconclusive results, infrared, ultraviolet or color filter photography may reveal the erased or obliterated material, or chemical treatment may be used.

A case concerning the theft in New York of bonds worth many thousands of dollars was considerably clarified by an examination in the FBI Laboratory of certain recovered bonds suspected of having altered serial numbers. Photographic and microscopic examinations of these bonds revealed that some of the numerals had been changed and with ink of similar color but different composition from that used to print the original numbers. Figure 28 is a photograph, slightly enlarged, of a serial number as it appeared on one of the stolen bonds. Figure 29 is a photomicrograph of the numeral "4" in this serial number, showing that it had actually been originally the numeral "1."

In another case, involving the theft of a leather jacket from a naval officer, the identifying name on the jacket

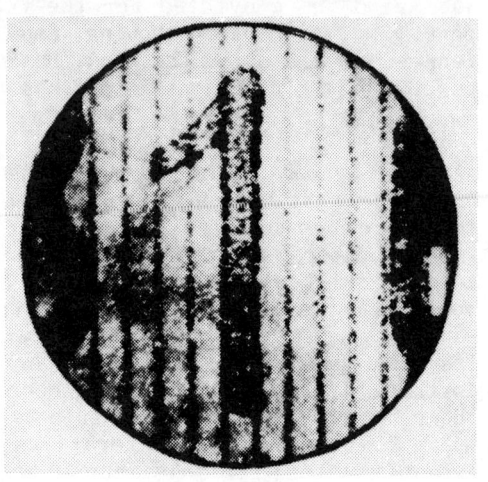

Figure 29

had been thoroughly scratched off the leather itself. However, ultraviolet photography brought out the name which had originally been stamped in gold. Figure 30 is a photograph of the obliterated area, and figure 31 shows the same area under ultraviolet light.

Still another case, this one concerning the identifying of an unknown body (a type of case in which the FBI Laboratory has often been called on for assistance), was also solved by the application of special photography to an obliteration on leather, but photography of a different sort from that used on the leather jacket. A woman's body was found in a Minnesota river, with no marks of identification. However, a leather knife sheath on the body bore a few faint and illegible traces of ink. The sheath was sent to the laboratory, and infrared photography disclosed a name by which she was later identified. Figure 32 is a portion of the sheath in ordinary light, and figure 33 is an infrared photograph of the same area.

Burning incriminating evidence would, to the criminal, seem to be a most effective way of destroying it. However, if the evidence is not completely burned to ashes, or if the charred remains are not crushed or pulverized, the original material may still be made legible. Extreme care should be taken in packing charred paper for submission to the FBI Laboratory. It should not be pulled apart (if it is in layers), moistened or flattened, but should be loosely packed in cotton in a strong box. In the laboratory the charred paper is made more pliable, then various photographic methods (including infrared photography which is unusually effective) are first attempted. If these fail, chemical methods may be tried.

An unusual case involving a charred document came about as the result of the death of an Army flier in a plane crash. Army investigators found in the wreckage a partially burned promissory note for several hundred dollars, payable to the dead flier, but with the signature charred beyond recognition. They sent the note to the FBI Laboratory, where it was possible by a combination of chemical and photographic methods to make the signature entirely legible.

The possibilities of uncovering various types of concealed clues in documentary evidence are almost endless, and depend to a great extent on the circumstances of the crime and the character of the material under examination. As examples of some of the many other kinds of incriminating evi-

Figure 30

Figure 31

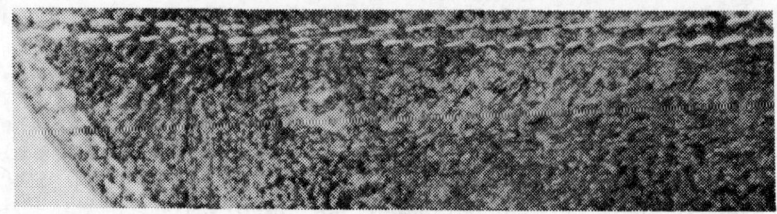

Figure 32

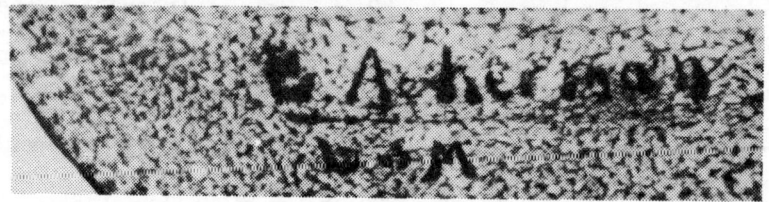

Figure 33

dence which a criminal might unconsciously leave, used carbon paper or typewriter ribbons may prove valuable in certain investigations. Special photography of the carbon paper, or, in some instances, the use of the paper itself as a "negative" from which photographic prints are made, will generally make the material on the paper readable unless the paper has been used so many times that it is entirely illegible. Likewise, a typewriter ribbon which has not been used very much may contain legible impressions which can be connected with a questioned document. The examination of typewriter ribbons has been discussed to some extent previously in connection with fraudulent checks. However, such an examination may also be valuable in other types of cases. For example, a typewritten extortion letter was received by an intended victim and was turned over to the FBI for investigation. A typewriter was found in the home of a suspect, and the investigator noted that the ribbon apparently had not been used much. This ribbon was removed from the typewriter and sent to the laboratory, where an examination disclosed the complete wording of the threatening letter clearly visible on the ribbon itself.

Handwriting Examination

Expert testimony based on handwriting analyses is now an approved, often essential, part of court trial procedure.

However, conditions were not always so favorable for this phase of crime detection. Even a few decades ago restrictions in a great many courts limited the scope of the document examination or the adequate presentation of handwriting testimony. The problems faced by the document expert under such conditions were extremely difficult, and sometimes resulted in ineffective testimony or no testimony at all. Now, however, the properly trained and qualified expert is accepted without bias in practically every court of law in the United States and its Territories as an essential witness in many types of cases.

This change has been brought about primarily by the great progress made in scientific study and analysis of handwriting during the past century. Out of this gradual accumulation of knowledge has come the realization that each person's writing--like each person's fingerprints--contains certain individual characteristics. This is the fundamental principle on which handwriting comparisons are based, and on which testimony is given in and accepted by courts of law

The basis of this principle is simple and logical. The natural and subconscious handwriting characteristics developed by the individual are a product both of the movements of the hand which writes and the mind which directs the writing. These two influences result in an infinite number of possible combinations of individual writing habits, each combination representing the sum of numerous physiological and psychological factors peculiar to the writer.

There may be a superficial and pictorial resemblance in the writings of two persons due to such influences as childhood training in similar styles of penmanship, the use of foreign letter formations, the "family" resemblance which sometimes occurs among writings of members of the same family, or a deliberate attempt to imitate the writing of another. Also, two documents written by one and the same person may appear to be "different" because of such factors as a change in writing conditions, the effects of illness or extreme fatigue, a long lapse of time between the two writings, or a deliberately assumed disguise.

However, detailed and expert analysis will as a rule reveal the hidden, automatic, entirely individual characteristics on which the document examiner bases his conclusion-- a definite scientific opinion based entirely on the elements contained in the documents themselves.

Anonymous Letters

This article on documentary examinations has previously discussed to some extent the examination of handwriting, particularly in connection with fraudulent checks and forgery cases. However, these types of cases usually involve signatures or very small amounts of writing. Examinations of larger amounts of handwritten material, such as evidence in anonymous letter cases, and the obtaining of proper known specimens for comparison purposes, may create additional problems. However, the previous discussion in this article relative to methods of obtaining known handwriting for comparison with checks generally applies equally well to other types of documentary evidence. The primary consideration to be remembered in obtaining any type of known evidence for comparison with questioned material is to *reproduce the original conditions of the preparation of the questioned material as nearly as possible.*

Disguised Writing

The problem of disguised writing frequently arises in anonymous letter cases. Rarely is there any attempt by the writer to imitate the writing of another person, but only to alter his own normal writing. These attempts at alteration usually destroy only the more obvious characteristics, leaving completely untouched the unconscious and inherent writing habits. One of the crudest and least effective (though often used) ways of disguise is a change in the slant of the writing. Changes in the size of the writing, extra flourishes in capital letters, angular formations of small letters--all these methods may alter the pictorial effect, but the basic characteristics remain unchanged. Even an attempt at disguise by writing with the hand other than that normally used is as a rule no more productive than any other form of disguise, since the same mind still guides the hand in the same basic writing habits. Some of the signs of disguised writing are unnatural line quality caused by slow or "drawing" movements, inconsistencies in letter formations, and an erratic overall appearance. The writing of a poorly educated person who is not accustomed to writing may appear to exhibit some of these same qualities. However, there is basic consistency in this type of writing which does not appear in disguised writing.

Handwriting Comparisons

Four anonymous letter cases may serve to illustrate some of the basic types of comparisons often encountered in handwriting analyses. The first case concerned an official of a Connecticut firm who received in the mail a package containing a crude homemade bomb and a handprinted threatening note. Known handprinting specimens of a suspect were sent to the FBI Laboratory for examination. In this case, the handprinting on the questioned note was highly disguised, whereas the known handprinting was written normally. However, the questioned handprinting consistently showed the same basic characteristics as the large amounts of known handprinting, both upper case and lower case, obtained from the suspect and the document examiner was able to state positively that this suspect had written the threatening note. Figure 34 is a portion of the questioned note, and figure 35 is a portion of the known printing in lower case letters.

Figure 34

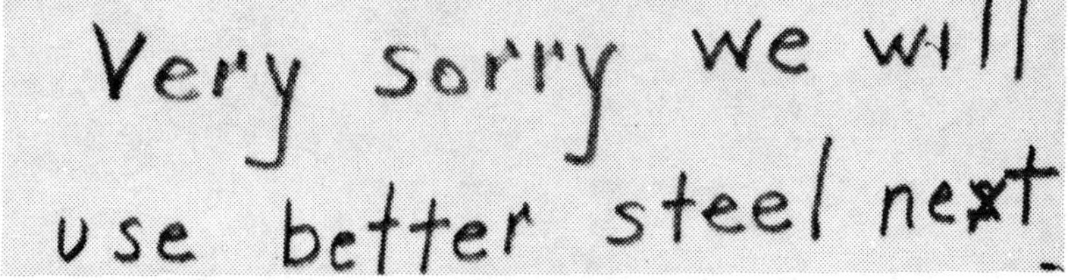

Figure 35

It is pointed out that this case actually involved
handprinting rather than handwriting, but the examination of
handprinting follows the same principles as the examination
of handwriting, since the same basic rules apply. It should
be noted, though, that a comparison of handwriting with
handprinting is rarely productive, since this type of comparison involves two entirely different styles of writing
and would as a rule be no more feasible than trying to com-
pare shorthand symbols with script writing. Therefore, when
the questioned material is handprinted, dictated known specimens should be obtained in both upper case and lower case
letters, or if dictated material cannot be obtained from a
suspect, a search should be made for samples of his handprinting rather than his handwriting.

The second anonymous letter case concerned a girl in
Florida who accused a man of threatening to kill her, and

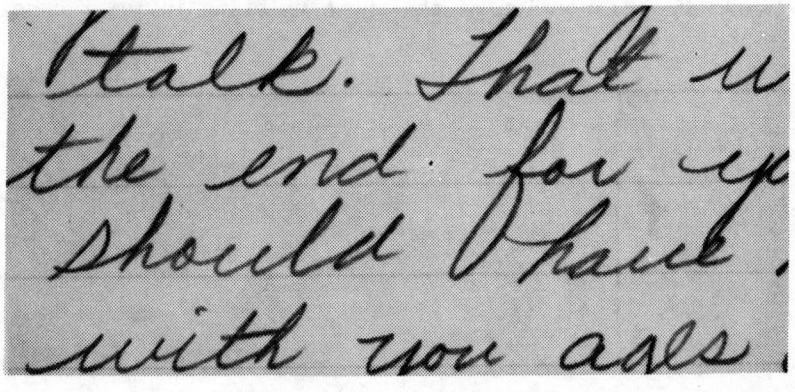

Figure 36

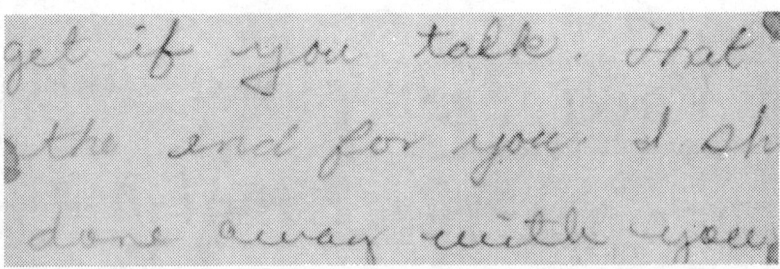

Figure 37

as proof displayed a threatening letter she said she had received in the mail, signed with his name. However, a document examination in the FBI Laboratory definitely eliminated the man as the writer of the letter. Then samples of the girl's writing both dictated and undictated, were submitted for comparison with the letter. The questioned writing showed no signs of disguise, other than the fact that it was rather large (perhaps an attempt to make it resemble a man's writing). However, the girl's dictated known writing was considerably disguised, and a study of her undictated writing (mostly personal correspondence) showed she had attempted several different styles of writing during the preceding few months. After a thorough analysis of all these writings, the threatening letter was positively identified as her work. Figure 36 is a portion of the questioned letter, and figure 37 is the disguised dictated writing of the girl.

In this case, the obtaining of undictated as well as dictated known writing of the girl was of great help to the document examiner. Often, when an attempt is made by a law enforcement officer to obtain dictated known specimens, the suspect may try to disguise his writing. By obtaining numerous specimens on separate sheets of paper, one after the other, and by removing each specimen from the suspect's sight as soon as it is completed, it is usually possible to eventually obtain representative samples of his normal writing, since it is extremely difficult to maintain a disguised manner of writing over a long period of time, or to continue a disguise consistent in its appearance with the previous disguised material. Another point which this case illustrates is the advisability of obtaining known specimens of the victim in anonymous letter cases whenever the investigation seems to justify this procedure, since instances of the "victim" writing the letter to himself or herself occur with surprising frequency.

The third anonymous letter case illustrates an unusual angle of this tendency in some persons deliberately to focus attention on themselves by methods which can hardly be considered legal (the same peculiarity which causes a pyromaniac to set a fire, then turn in the alarm himself). This case began with a crudely handprinted anonymous note found in a mail box in Michigan. The note advised that a man's body had just been found in a "hobo camp" nearby. An immediate search of the area located the body of a murdered man.

On the chance that the murderer himself might have written the note, a comparison of the questioned handprinting with known handprinting of a suspect was requested of the FBI Laboratory, and a positive identification was made. Though the suspect had at first flatly denied any previous knowledge of the body, he finally confessed when told of the results of the laboratory examination. He said he had been so upset when he returned to the scene of the murder the following day and found the body still there that he had written the note. In this particular case, the crudity of the

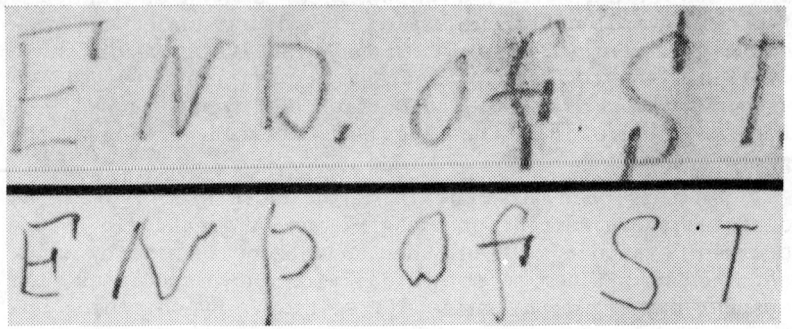

Figure 38

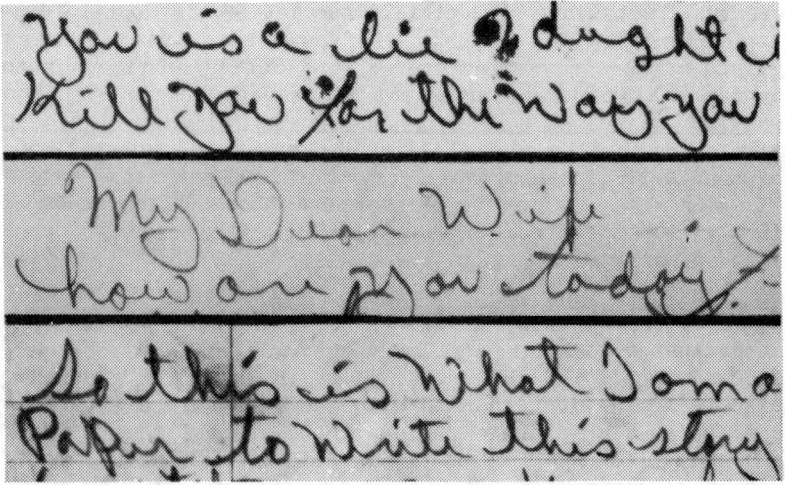

Figure 39

questioned handprinting would appear at first sight to be due to an attempt at disguise, yet a thorough examination showed the characteristics to be natural and individual, and perfectly consistent with the characteristics in the known printing. Figure 38 shows small portions of the anonymous note (upper) and the known printing (lower).

The fourth anonymous letter case used here for illustrative purposes concerned a woman found murdered in Georgia. By the body was a threatening letter signed with the name of one of her acquaintances, whom investigation promptly eliminated as a suspect. Several circumstances pointed to the woman's husband as the murderer, and when his known writing was sent to the FBI Laboratory he was positively identified as the writer of the letter to which he had signed another man's name. He was convicted of the murder and sentenced to die. However, about a month after the trial a newspaper received a letter signed "Ziggy," confessing to the murder, and stating that the woman's husband was entirely innocent. "Ziggy" also stated that his handwriting would be found to be exactly like the husband's handwriting. This letter was also sent to the FBI Laboratory, and the writing was identified not only with the writing on the original threatening letter but also with the known writing of the husband. The "Ziggy" letter had obviously been smuggled out of jail by one of the husband's visitors in a desperate attempt to save him from the electric chair. Figure 39 shows small portions of the threatening letter, the known writing of the husband, and the "Ziggy" letter.

The peculiar feature of this case was that these three letters, each signed with the name of a "different" person, showed no signs of any attempts at disguise in any of the writings. The murderer thus displayed a complete ignorance of the possibilities of handwriting comparisons, and assumed that since it was supposedly "impossible" for him to mail a letter while he was in jail, any identification of his known writing with the "Ziggy" letter would not be accepted. However, the fundamental principle of handwriting analysis--that each person's writing contains its own individual characteristics--still remains constant.

The purpose of this article has been twofold--to give some idea of the wide range of scientific examinations that can be made in the field of document work, and to point out to law enforcement officers the possibilities of these examinations in assisting their own investigations.